★Richard Simmons MAD LIBS®

by Brandon T. Snider

MAD LIBS
An imprint of Penguin Random House LLC, New York

First published in the United States of America by Mad Libs,
an imprint of Penguin Random House LLC, New York, 2022

Mad Libs format copyright © 2022 by Penguin Random House LLC

Concept created by Roger Price & Leonard Stern

© Jemini LLC

Visit us online at penguinrandomhouse.com.

Printed in the United States of America

ISBN 9780593519257
1 3 5 7 9 10 8 6 4 2
COMR

MAD LIBS

INSTRUCTIONS

MAD LIBS® is a game for people who don't like games!
It can be played by one, two, three, four, or forty.

● RIDICULOUSLY SIMPLE DIRECTIONS

In this tablet you will find stories containing blank spaces where words
are left out. One player, the READER, selects one of these stories. The
READER does not tell anyone what the story is about. Instead, he/she asks
the other players, the WRITERS, to give him/her words. These words are
used to fill in the blank spaces in the story.

● TO PLAY

The READER asks each WRITER in turn to call out a word—an adjective or
a noun or whatever the space calls for—and uses them to fill in the blank
spaces in the story. The result is a MAD LIBS® game.

When the READER then reads the completed MAD LIBS® game to the other
players, they will discover that they have written a story that is fantastic,
screamingly funny, shocking, silly, crazy, or just plain dumb—depending
upon which words each WRITER called out.

● EXAMPLE (*Before* and *After*)

"_____!" he said _____
  EXCLAMATION   ADVERB

as he jumped into his convertible _____ and
                                                              NOUN

drove off with his _____ wife.
                              ADJECTIVE

"_____OUCH_____!" he said _____HAPPILY_____
  EXCLAMATION   ADVERB

as he jumped into his convertible _____CAT_____ and
                                                              NOUN

drove off with his _____BRAVE_____ wife.
                              ADJECTIVE

In case you have forgotten what adjectives, adverbs, nouns, and verbs are, here is a quick review:

An ADJECTIVE describes something or somebody. *Lumpy, soft, ugly, messy,* and *short* are adjectives.

An ADVERB tells how something is done. It modifies a verb and usually ends in "ly." *Modestly, stupidly, greedily,* and *carefully* are adverbs.

A NOUN is the name of a person, place, or thing. *Sidewalk, umbrella, bridle, bathtub,* and *nose* are nouns.

A VERB is an action word. *Run, pitch, jump,* and *swim* are verbs. Put the verbs in past tense if the directions say PAST TENSE. *Ran, pitched, jumped,* and *swam* are verbs in the past tense.

When we ask for A PLACE, we mean any sort of place: a country or city (*Spain, Cleveland*) or a room (*bathroom, kitchen*).

An EXCLAMATION or SILLY WORD is any sort of funny sound, gasp, grunt, or outcry, like *Wow!, Ouch!, Whomp!, Ick!,* and *Gadzooks!*

When we ask for specific words, like a NUMBER, a COLOR, an ANIMAL, or a PART OF THE BODY, we mean a word that is one of those things, like *seven, blue, horse,* or *head.*

When we ask for a PLURAL, it means more than one. For example, *cat* pluralized is *cats.*

MAD LIBS® is fun to play with friends, but you can also play it by yourself! To begin with, DO NOT look at the story on the page below. Fill in the blanks on this page with the words called for. Then, using the words you have selected, fill in the blank spaces in the story.

Now you've created your own hilarious MAD LIBS® game!

EXERCISE ICON

NUMBER _____

VERB _____

ADJECTIVE _____

LAST NAME _____

ADJECTIVE _____

TYPE OF FOOD _____

OCCUPATION _____

VERB ENDING IN "ING" _____

NOUN _____

CITY _____

SILLY NAME _____

PART OF THE BODY (PLURAL) _____

ADJECTIVE _____

CELEBRITY _____

PLURAL NOUN _____

NUMBER _____

NOUN _____

MAD LIBS

EXERCISE ICON

"Number _____ , _____ yourself!" said Richard
            NUMBER   VERB

Simmons, the famously _____ fitness instructor. He was
                            ADJECTIVE

born Milton Teagle _____ in New Orleans, Louisiana,
                        LAST NAME

and raised in the city's _____ Quarter. As a young man,
                              ADJECTIVE

Simmons was a/an _____ _____ , selling his wares
                   TYPE OF FOOD   OCCUPATION

on street corners and _____ with customers. Though
                       VERB ENDING IN "ING"

full of humor, young Richard struggled with his _____ .
                                                      NOUN

As he got older, he wanted to help others like himself, so he

moved to the bright lights of _____ and opened a gym
                                    CITY

called _____ . Richard's energetic classes made people
          SILLY NAME

shake their _____ ! His _____ personality
            PART OF THE BODY (PLURAL)   ADJECTIVE

soon turned Richard into a star. He appeared on *The Tonight Show*

with _____ as well as infomercials selling his workout
         CELEBRITY

_____ and meal plans. That little boy from Louisiana
   PLURAL NOUN

also went on to author _____ books. Now he's celebrated
                            NUMBER

throughout the world as the _____ saint!
                                  NOUN

From RICHARD SIMMONS MAD LIBS® • © Jemini LLC.
Published by Mad Libs, an imprint of Penguin Random House LLC, 2022

MAD LIBS® is fun to play with friends, but you can also play it by yourself! To begin with, DO NOT look at the story on the page below. Fill in the blanks on this page with the words called for. Then, using the words you have selected, fill in the blank spaces in the story.

Now you've created your own hilarious MAD LIBS® game!

PARTY OFF THE POUNDS

FIRST NAME _____

VERB _____

A PLACE _____

NOUN _____

ADJECTIVE _____

ARTICLE OF CLOTHING (PLURAL) _____

PART OF THE BODY _____

NOUN _____

VERB ENDING IN "ING" _____

TYPE OF FOOD _____

PLURAL NOUN _____

ADJECTIVE _____

TYPE OF LIQUID _____

VERB _____

VERB ENDING IN "ING" _____

PART OF THE BODY _____

CELEBRITY _____

TYPE OF LIQUID _____

MAD LIBS®

PARTY OFF THE POUNDS

_____ is hosting a/an _____ -out extravaganza!
FIRST NAME   VERB

Where: (the) _____
A PLACE

When: 2:00 p.m. till the _____ strikes midnight
NOUN

Tired of feeling _____? Are your _____
ADJECTIVE   ARTICLE OF CLOTHING (PLURAL)

a little snug around the _____? Well, then Richard has
PART OF THE BODY

a/an _____ for you! He's throwing a party that will have you
NOUN

_____ like never before. You won't find _____
VERB ENDING IN "ING"   TYPE OF FOOD

at this get-together, but you _will_ find _____ who want
PLURAL NOUN

to see you _____ and thriving. So, throw on your best
ADJECTIVE

_____-pants and get ready to _____! Richard
TYPE OF LIQUID   VERB

will be _____ his _____ off. If you're
VERB ENDING IN "ING"   PART OF THE BODY

lucky, _____ might even pop over and sing their newest
CELEBRITY

hit. Stop on by and don't forget to bring your _____
TYPE OF LIQUID

bottle. You're gonna need it!

From RICHARD SIMMONS MAD LIBS® • © Jemini LLC.
Published by Mad Libs, an imprint of Penguin Random House LLC, 2022

MAD LIBS® is fun to play with friends, but you can also play it by yourself! To begin with, DO NOT look at the story on the page below. Fill in the blanks on this page with the words called for. Then, using the words you have selected, fill in the blank spaces in the story.

Now you've created your own hilarious MAD LIBS® game!

OH, HAPPY DAY

SILLY WORD _____

ARTICLE OF CLOTHING _____

VERB _____

ADJECTIVE _____

VERB (PAST TENSE) _____

NOUN _____

VERB ENDING IN "ING" _____

OCCUPATION _____

PLURAL NOUN _____

COLOR _____

NUMBER _____

FIRST NAME _____

ANIMAL _____

TYPE OF FOOD _____

PART OF THE BODY _____

CELEBRITY _____

EXCLAMATION _____

OH, HAPPY DAY

Terry: Hey, _____ ! Are you ready for our workout with
SILLY WORD

Richard?! I just bought a brand-new _____ and
ARTICLE OF CLOTHING

I'm itching to _____ it!
VERB

Geri: I'm a little _____ . The last time I _____
ADJECTIVE   _VERB (PAST TENSE)_

with a trainer, she broke my _____ to live.
NOUN

Terry: Richard is all about positive _____ . He's the
VERB ENDING IN "ING"

best _____ I've ever had!
OCCUPATION

Geri: Do I have to lift _____ ?
PLURAL NOUN

Terry: Yes, but they're _____ and only _____ pounds.
COLOR   _NUMBER_

C'mon! We can go to _____'s _____ Shack
FIRST NAME   _ANIMAL_

afterward for _____ as a treat.
TYPE OF FOOD

Geri: I don't know. I think I have to braid my _____
PART OF THE BODY

instead.

Terry: I heard _____ might stop by.
CELEBRITY

Geri: What?! _____ ! Okay, I'm in!
EXCLAMATION

MAD LIBS® is fun to play with friends, but you can also play it by yourself! To begin with, DO NOT look at the story on the page below. Fill in the blanks on this page with the words called for. Then, using the words you have selected, fill in the blank spaces in the story.

Now you've created your own hilarious MAD LIBS® game!

DEAL-A-MEAL

VERB ENDING IN "ING" _____

ADJECTIVE _____

TYPE OF FOOD _____

ADJECTIVE _____

TYPE OF LIQUID _____

PLURAL NOUN _____

NOUN _____

ADJECTIVE _____

ADVERB _____

TYPE OF CONTAINER _____

NUMBER _____

VERB _____

PLURAL NOUN _____

ADJECTIVE _____

TYPE OF FOOD _____

EXCLAMATION _____

A PLACE _____

MAD LIBS®

DEAL-A-MEAL

_____ doesn't have to be scary! Check out this recipe
VERB ENDING IN "ING"

for _____ raisin _____ , crafted with love by
ADJECTIVE   TYPE OF FOOD

Richard himself.

- First, combine one-quarter cup of _____-fashioned
  ADJECTIVE

  oats, one-third cup of boiling _____ , and one
  TYPE OF LIQUID

  tablespoon of _____ into a bowl.
  PLURAL NOUN

- Place the bowl into your _____ and cook it on
  NOUN

  _____ heat for two minutes, then stir _____ .
  ADJECTIVE   ADVERB

  Place the _____ back in the microwave for
  TYPE OF CONTAINER

  _____ minutes. _____ again.
  NUMBER   VERB

- Then, sprinkle in two teaspoons of chopped _____ .
  PLURAL NOUN

- For a change, use a/an _____ fruit like a banana or a
  ADJECTIVE

  cup of _____ instead of raisins.
  TYPE OF FOOD

This low-calorie snack will have you shouting "_____!"
                                              EXCLAMATION

from (the) _____ .
           A PLACE

MAD LIBS® is fun to play with friends, but you can also play it by yourself! To begin with, DO NOT look at the story on the page below. Fill in the blanks on this page with the words called for. Then, using the words you have selected, fill in the blank spaces in the story.

Now you've created your own hilarious MAD LIBS® game!

LOVE YOURSELF AND WIN

PERSON IN ROOM _____

VERB ENDING IN "ING" _____

TYPE OF EVENT _____

PART OF THE BODY _____

OCCUPATION _____

NOUN _____

LAST NAME _____

NUMBER _____

TYPE OF FOOD _____

TYPE OF LIQUID _____

ARTICLE OF CLOTHING (PLURAL) _____

PLURAL NOUN _____

ADJECTIVE _____

FIRST NAME _____

PART OF THE BODY (PLURAL) _____

VERB _____

ANIMAL _____

NUMBER _____

How good is _____ at inspiring people? Let these
PERSON IN ROOM

testimonials tell the tale:

Linda: My first day _____ with Richard was nerve-
VERB ENDING IN "ING"

racking! I'd never been to a/an _____ before. He
TYPE OF EVENT

saw me struggling, took me by the _____, and said,
PART OF THE BODY

"You've got this, you're a/an _____!" Those words changed
OCCUPATION

my _____!
NOUN

Mr. _____ : _____ months ago I was eating too
LAST NAME　　　NUMBER

much _____, drinking a lot of _____, and
TYPE OF FOOD　　　TYPE OF LIQUID

didn't feel good in my _____. I felt like a
ARTICLE OF CLOTHING (PLURAL)

bucket of _____ until I took Richard's class. Now I'm
PLURAL NOUN

more _____ than ever!
ADJECTIVE

_____ : Richard had us grab our _____
FIRST NAME　　　PART OF THE BODY (PLURAL)

and _____! I felt like a/an _____. And I loved it!
VERB　　　ANIMAL

Best _____ minutes of my life.
NUMBER

— From RICHARD SIMMONS MAD LIBS® • © Jemini LLC.
Published by Mad Libs, an imprint of Penguin Random House LLC, 2022

MAD LIBS® is fun to play with friends, but you can also play it by yourself! To begin with, DO NOT look at the story on the page below. Fill in the blanks on this page with the words called for. Then, using the words you have selected, fill in the blank spaces in the story.

Now you've created your own hilarious MAD LIBS® game!

REACH!

FIRST NAME _____

ADJECTIVE _____

SILLY WORD _____

NUMBER _____

VERB ENDING IN "ING" _____

ADJECTIVE _____

PERSON IN ROOM _____

ANIMAL _____

NOUN _____

ARTICLE OF CLOTHING _____

PART OF THE BODY _____

VERB ENDING IN "ING" _____

TYPE OF FOOD _____

PLURAL NOUN _____

TYPE OF LIQUID _____

SOMETHING ALIVE _____

CELEBRITY _____

PART OF THE BODY (PLURAL) _____

MAD LIBS

REACH!

Dear _____,
　　　　　FIRST NAME

It's time for my _____ check-in, and things have been kind
　　　　　　　　　　ADJECTIVE

of _____. Getting up at _____ o'clock and
　　　SILLY WORD　　　　　　　　　　　　NUMBER

_____ every morning is not my favorite, but I feel
VERB ENDING IN "ING"

stronger every day—which reminds me of a/an _____
　　　　　　　　　　　　　　　　　　　　　　　ADJECTIVE

story, actually! Yesterday, I was walking _____, my pet
　　　　　　　　　　　　　　　　　　　　PERSON IN ROOM

_____, and when I reached down to pick up her
　　ANIMAL

_____, my _____ ripped open! I guess my
　　NOUN　　　　　ARTICLE OF CLOTHING

_____ is getting firm from all the _____
PART OF THE BODY　　　　　　　　　　　　　VERB ENDING IN "ING"

that I'm doing in my exercise class, ha-ha. Afterward, as a reward

for good progress, I had a bowl of _____ with some
　　　　　　　　　　　　　　　　　TYPE OF FOOD

_____ sprinkled on top and a glass of fresh orange
　　PLURAL NOUN

_____. Changing my lifestyle and way of eating makes
　TYPE OF LIQUID

me feel like a spring _____ again. If I stay on track, I'll
　　　　　　　　　　SOMETHING ALIVE

look like _____ by the holidays! _____
　　　　　CELEBRITY　　　　　　　　　　　　PART OF THE BODY (PLURAL)

crossed.

MAD LIBS® is fun to play with friends, but you can also play it by yourself! To begin with, DO NOT look at the story on the page below. Fill in the blanks on this page with the words called for. Then, using the words you have selected, fill in the blank spaces in the story.

Now you've created your own hilarious MAD LIBS® game!

SIMMONS HOUSE RULES

TYPE OF LIQUID _____

PART OF THE BODY _____

CELEBRITY _____

ARTICLE OF CLOTHING (PLURAL) _____

A PLACE _____

OCCUPATION _____

PLURAL NOUN _____

VERB ENDING IN "ING" _____

ADVERB _____

VERB _____

PART OF THE BODY _____

TYPE OF FOOD _____

NOUN _____

EXCLAMATION _____

FIRST NAME _____

ADJECTIVE _____

SIMMONS HOUSE RULES

If you want to work out with Richard, you'll have to follow his list of dos and don'ts.

- **DO** bring a bottle of _____ with you. You'll need

TYPE OF LIQUID
  it after shaking your _____ to _____'s

PART OF THE BODY   CELEBRITY
  newest bop.

- **DON'T** leave your sweaty _____ lying

ARTICLE OF CLOTHING (PLURAL)
  around. The studio is not your _____, and Richard is

A PLACE
  not your _____ .

OCCUPATION

- **DO** be kind to other _____. If you see someone

PLURAL NOUN
  _____, _____ help them out.

VERB ENDING IN "ING"   ADVERB

- **DON'T** eat a big meal before you _____ or you'll get

VERB
  a/an _____-ache. Save your _____

PART OF THE BODY   TYPE OF FOOD
  dinner till after your workout.

- **DO** ask for a/an _____ if you find yourself struggling.

NOUN
  Say, "_____, _____! Could I please get

EXCLAMATION   FIRST NAME
  some _____ help?"

ADJECTIVE

From RICHARD SIMMONS MAD LIBS® • © Jemini LLC.
Published by Mad Libs, an imprint of Penguin Random House LLC, 2022

MAD LIBS® is fun to play with friends, but you can also play it by yourself! To begin with, DO NOT look at the story on the page below. Fill in the blanks on this page with the words called for. Then, using the words you have selected, fill in the blank spaces in the story.

Now you've created your own hilarious MAD LIBS® game!

GROOVIN' IN THE HOUSE

PART OF THE BODY _____

NOUN _____

VERB ENDING IN "ING" _____

ADJECTIVE _____

A PLACE _____

EXCLAMATION _____

TYPE OF EVENT _____

PLURAL NOUN _____

ARTICLE OF CLOTHING (PLURAL) _____

COLOR _____

ADJECTIVE _____

VEHICLE _____

OCCUPATION _____

VERB ENDING IN "ING" _____

MAD LIBS

GROOVIN' IN THE HOUSE

Get up and shake your _____ ,

PART OF THE BODY

there's no _____ to waste.

NOUN

_____ till the _____ light

VERB ENDING IN "ING"   ADJECTIVE

will have you feeling spaced.

Come on down to Richard's _____ ,

A PLACE

shout " _____ ," and be free.

EXCLAMATION

This _____ will make you shake

TYPE OF EVENT

for all the _____ to see.

PLURAL NOUN

Let the music move you,

leave your _____ on the floor.

ARTICLE OF CLOTHING (PLURAL)

_____ lights and _____ sounds

COLOR   ADJECTIVE

will have you wanting more.

So, hop in your _____ and come on down.

VEHICLE

Bring a/an _____ or bring a spouse.

OCCUPATION

Everyone is welcome

when you're _____ in Richard's house.

VERB ENDING IN "ING"

From RICHARD SIMMONS MAD LIBS® • © Jemini LLC.
Published by Mad Libs, an imprint of Penguin Random House LLC, 2022

MAD LIBS® is fun to play with friends, but you can also play it by yourself! To begin with, DO NOT look at the story on the page below. Fill in the blanks on this page with the words called for. Then, using the words you have selected, fill in the blank spaces in the story.

Now you've created your own hilarious MAD LIBS® game!

CRUISE 2 LOSE

SILLY WORD _____

ADJECTIVE _____

ADVERB _____

PLURAL NOUN _____

VERB ENDING IN "ING" _____

COUNTRY _____

NUMBER _____

CITY _____

VEHICLE _____

NOUN _____

OCCUPATION _____

PART OF THE BODY _____

ARTICLE OF CLOTHING _____

ADJECTIVE _____

VERB ENDING IN "ING" _____

TYPE OF LIQUID _____

TYPE OF FOOD _____

NOUN _____

_____, me mateys! Are you ready to set sail on the
_____SILLY WORD_____

_____ seas? Richard Simmons _____ invites you
ADJECTIVE   ADVERB

on a fitness journey filled with _____, food, and
                                          PLURAL NOUN

_____. All aboard the _____ *Princess*! For
VERB ENDING IN "ING"   COUNTRY

_____ days, you'll cruise around the globe, visiting cities like
NUMBER

_____ while exercising in the _____'s luxurious
CITY   VEHICLE

_____. Worried about getting seasick? Don't be! We've got
NOUN

a/an _____ on board in case your _____ feels
OCCUPATION   PART OF THE BODY

wonky. And don't forget to bring a bathing _____.
                                            ARTICLE OF CLOTHING

You'll want to check out one of the _____ pools when
                                          ADJECTIVE

you're not _____ to the oldies. The _____
VERB ENDING IN "ING"   TYPE OF LIQUID

is quite cool and refreshing after a long day. At night, enjoy the

healthy _____ buffet and indulge. Join us on the
TYPE OF FOOD

_____ of a lifetime!
NOUN

MAD LIBS® is fun to play with friends, but you can also play it by yourself! To begin with, DO NOT look at the story on the page below. Fill in the blanks on this page with the words called for. Then, using the words you have selected, fill in the blank spaces in the story.

Now you've created your own hilarious MAD LIBS® game!

WICKED WORKOUT

VERB ENDING IN "ING" _____

ANIMAL _____

A PLACE _____

PART OF THE BODY (PLURAL) _____

VERB _____

NUMBER _____

NOUN _____

ADJECTIVE _____

PART OF THE BODY (PLURAL) _____

ADVERB _____

ADJECTIVE _____

VERB ENDING IN "ING" _____

PART OF THE BODY _____

NUMBER _____

ADJECTIVE _____

SILLY WORD _____

NOUN _____

ANIMAL _____

These exercises will get you _____ and ready for

VERB ENDING IN "ING"

action!

- For the _____ crawl, find a/an _____ that's long

ANIMAL   A PLACE

  and wide. Then get on your hands and _____

PART OF THE BODY (PLURAL)

  and _____ down and back. _____ sets should

VERB   NUMBER

  strengthen your _____ in no time.

NOUN

- _____ kicks are fun and simple. Lie down on your

ADJECTIVE

  back with your _____ in the air. _____

PART OF THE BODY (PLURAL)   ADVERB

  kick your legs and feel your abs get _____.

ADJECTIVE

- _____ jacks work every part of the body, even

VERB ENDING IN "ING"

  the _____. Just _____ minutes a day will have

PART OF THE BODY   NUMBER

  you feeling _____.

ADJECTIVE

Other exercises like _____, _____ climbers, and

SILLY WORD   NOUN

_____ kicks can also help get your blood pumping!

ANIMAL

From RICHARD SIMMONS MAD LIBS® • © Jemini LLC.

Published by Mad Libs, an imprint of Penguin Random House LLC, 2022

MAD LIBS® is fun to play with friends, but you can also play it by yourself! To begin with, DO NOT look at the story on the page below. Fill in the blanks on this page with the words called for. Then, using the words you have selected, fill in the blank spaces in the story.

Now you've created your own hilarious MAD LIBS® game!

TOAST OF LATE NIGHT

LAST NAME _____

CELEBRITY _____

VERB (PAST TENSE) _____

ADVERB _____

TYPE OF FOOD _____

A PLACE _____

ANIMAL _____

PART OF THE BODY _____

ARTICLE OF CLOTHING _____

VERB (PAST TENSE) _____

TYPE OF LIQUID _____

OCCUPATION _____

PLURAL NOUN _____

ARTICLE OF CLOTHING _____

PLURAL NOUN _____

SILLY WORD _____

PART OF THE BODY _____

ADJECTIVE _____

MAD LIBS

TOAST OF LATE NIGHT

"Please welcome Richard _____!" said the host of *Late*
_{LAST NAME}

Night with _____. The crowd went wild! The audience
_{CELEBRITY}

_____ as Richard _____ raced through the
_{VERB (PAST TENSE)}   _{ADVERB}

TV studio, handing out _____. He tiptoed into
_{TYPE OF FOOD}

(the) _____ and took a seat next to the host. "Hello, my
_{A PLACE}

little _____!" Richard cooed. The host tapped Richard
_{ANIMAL}

on the _____. "Do you know you're wearing a/an
_{PART OF THE BODY}

_____, Richard?" he asked. "I'm glad you finally
_{ARTICLE OF CLOTHING}

_____," Richard giggled, and took a drink of his
_{VERB (PAST TENSE)}

_____. "I'm just a humble _____. I bring
_{TYPE OF LIQUID}   _{OCCUPATION}

_____ to people and make them feel great. The
_{PLURAL NOUN}

_____ is just for show," he said with a wink. The host
_{ARTICLE OF CLOTHING}

grinned. "Any advice for the _____ out there?" he asked.
_{PLURAL NOUN}

Richard looked directly into the camera. "_____! Shake
_{SILLY WORD}

your _____! And always remember to have a/an
_{PART OF THE BODY}

_____ time!"
_{ADJECTIVE}

From RICHARD SIMMONS MAD LIBS® • © Jemini LLC.
Published by Mad Libs, an imprint of Penguin Random House LLC, 2022

MAD LIBS® is fun to play with friends, but you can also play it by yourself! To begin with, DO NOT look at the story on the page below. Fill in the blanks on this page with the words called for. Then, using the words you have selected, fill in the blank spaces in the story.

Now you've created your own hilarious MAD LIBS® game!

SWEATIN' TO THE OLDIES

NOUN _____

PLURAL NOUN _____

ADJECTIVE _____

PERSON IN ROOM _____

CELEBRITY _____

NUMBER _____

PLURAL NOUN _____

PART OF THE BODY _____

COLOR _____

ARTICLE OF CLOTHING _____

ANIMAL _____

VERB ENDING IN "ING" _____

A PLACE _____

ADJECTIVE _____

VERB _____

EXCLAMATION _____

ADJECTIVE _____

VERB _____

MAD LIBS

SWEATIN' TO THE OLDIES

The _____ you've been waiting for has finally arrived!
　　　　　NOUN

Sweatin' to the _____ : *The* _____ *Collection* has
　　　　　　　　　PLURAL NOUN　　　　　ADJECTIVE

all your favorite workouts. _____ and _____
　　　　　　　　　　　　　PERSON IN ROOM　　　　　CELEBRITY

have selected the best of the best, and they're bringing them right

to you! For the low price of _____ dollars, you'll get four
　　　　　　　　　　　　　　NUMBER

_____ containing exercise routines that'll get your
PLURAL NOUN

_____ moving, featuring hits like "Devil with a/an
PART OF THE BODY

_____ _____ On," "Hungry Like the
COLOR　　　　　ARTICLE OF CLOTHING

_____," " _____ in (the) _____," and
ANIMAL　　　　VERB ENDING IN "ING"　　　　A PLACE

" _____ Girls Don't _____." But, _____,
ADJECTIVE　　　　　　　　VERB　　　　　EXCLAMATION

there's more! The first hundred orders get a limited-edition remix

of " _____ Girls Don't _____." Call now before
ADJECTIVE　　　　　　　VERB

it's too late!

From RICHARD SIMMONS MAD LIBS® • © Jemini LLC.
Published by Mad Libs, an imprint of Penguin Random House LLC, 2022

MAD LIBS® is fun to play with friends, but you can also play it by yourself! To begin with, DO NOT look at the story on the page below. Fill in the blanks on this page with the words called for. Then, using the words you have selected, fill in the blank spaces in the story.

Now you've created your own hilarious MAD LIBS® game!

WORDS TO LIVE BY

NOUN _____

VERB _____

FIRST NAME _____

PART OF THE BODY _____

A PLACE _____

PERSON IN ROOM _____

NOUN _____

VERB _____

ADJECTIVE _____

VERB _____

PART OF THE BODY _____

TYPE OF FOOD _____

VERB _____

SOMETHING ALIVE _____

PLURAL NOUN _____

ANIMAL _____

ADJECTIVE _____

MAD LIBS®

WORDS TO LIVE BY

We all need a little _____ sometimes. Take a good look in the
                        NOUN

mirror and repeat this list of inspirational words to _____ by.
                                                         VERB

— _____
                        FIRST NAME

- Always lead with your _____ , even if it takes you to
                         PART OF THE BODY

  (the) _____ .
          A PLACE

- Hey, _____ ! You're one special _____ , and
        PERSON IN ROOM   NOUN

  you deserve to _____ !
                    VERB

- You are _____ and unique. Never forget that.
            ADJECTIVE

- _____ yourself, move your _____ , and don't
    VERB   PART OF THE BODY

  eat too much _____ .
                 TYPE OF FOOD

- Today I will _____ like my _____ depends
                VERB   SOMETHING ALIVE

  on it. Because it does!

- Be kind to _____ and yourself.
               PLURAL NOUN

- I am like a/an _____ , fierce and _____ .
                  ANIMAL   ADJECTIVE

MAD LIBS® is fun to play with friends, but you can also play it by yourself! To begin with, DO NOT look at the story on the page below. Fill in the blanks on this page with the words called for. Then, using the words you have selected, fill in the blank spaces in the story.

Now you've created your own hilarious MAD LIBS® game!

LOOKIN' GOOD!

ADJECTIVE _____

OCCUPATION _____

ARTICLE OF CLOTHING _____

VERB ENDING IN "ING" _____

COLOR _____

ANIMAL _____

TYPE OF FOOD _____

PLURAL NOUN _____

ADJECTIVE _____

TYPE OF EVENT _____

VERB ENDING IN "ING" _____

TYPE OF LIQUID _____

SILLY WORD _____

VERB _____

TYPE OF CONTAINER _____

PERSON IN ROOM _____

NUMBER _____

PLURAL NOUN _____

MAD LIBS
LOOKIN' GOOD!

Here's a list of all the _____ workout swag you'll need to
ADJECTIVE

begin your fitness journey like a/an _____ .
OCCUPATION

- First, find yourself a comfortable _____ to wear
ARTICLE OF CLOTHING

when you're _____ . Maybe choose something in
VERB ENDING IN "ING"

_____ or, perhaps, _____ print?
COLOR   ANIMAL

- Don't fill up on _____ before exercising. Instead,
TYPE OF FOOD

grab a couple of snack-size _____ in case you feel
PLURAL NOUN

_____ *after* your sweaty _____ .
ADJECTIVE   TYPE OF EVENT

- _____ will surely make you thirsty, so bring a/an
VERB ENDING IN "ING"

_____ bottle and keep it filled. Make sure it has
TYPE OF LIQUID

a filter to protect against _____ chemicals.
SILLY WORD

- How are you going to _____ all this stuff? With a
VERB

sturdy _____ , of course. Preferably one that has
TYPE OF CONTAINER

_____ 's face on it. Toss _____ _____
PERSON IN ROOM   NUMBER   PLURAL NOUN

in there, and you'll be good to go!

From RICHARD SIMMONS MAD LIBS® • © Jemini LLC.
Published by Mad Libs, an imprint of Penguin Random House LLC, 2022

MAD LIBS® is fun to play with friends, but you can also play it by yourself! To begin with, DO NOT look at the story on the page below. Fill in the blanks on this page with the words called for. Then, using the words you have selected, fill in the blank spaces in the story.

Now you've created your own hilarious MAD LIBS® game!

IN HIS OWN WORDS

PERSON IN ROOM _____

VERB ENDING IN "ING" _____

EXCLAMATION _____

NOUN _____

ADJECTIVE _____

TYPE OF FOOD _____

TYPE OF LIQUID _____

PART OF THE BODY _____

ADJECTIVE _____

VERB _____

PLURAL NOUN _____

SOMETHING ALIVE _____

OCCUPATION _____

CELEBRITY _____

ADVERB _____

NOUN _____

MAD LIBS®

IN HIS OWN WORDS

Hello, _____ . Yes, *you.* I've seen you _____
PERSON IN ROOM   VERB ENDING IN "ING"

and wanted to take a moment to say, _____! My
         EXCLAMATION

_____ is just like yours, and I know how hard it can be
NOUN

when you don't feel very _____ . Years ago, I would eat
       ADJECTIVE

_____ for breakfast and wash it down with some
TYPE OF FOOD

_____ . My _____ hurt, but I didn't care.
TYPE OF LIQUID   PART OF THE BODY

It felt _____ . That was all that mattered to me. But
     ADJECTIVE

then I learned to _____ myself. Then, all those nasty
       VERB

_____ telling me that I wasn't worth it, that I wasn't
PLURAL NOUN

a/an _____ , suddenly disappeared. I became my own
    SOMETHING ALIVE

_____ , and *you* can, too. You don't need to be like
OCCUPATION

_____ or anyone else. Just treat people _____ and
CELEBRITY   ADVERB

be the best _____ you can be. I believe in you.
     NOUN

—Richard

From RICHARD SIMMONS MAD LIBS® • © Jemini LLC.
Published by Mad Libs, an imprint of Penguin Random House LLC, 2022

MAD LIBS® is fun to play with friends, but you can also play it by yourself! To begin with, DO NOT look at the story on the page below. Fill in the blanks on this page with the words called for. Then, using the words you have selected, fill in the blank spaces in the story.

Now you've created your own hilarious MAD LIBS® game!

FITNESS FIESTA

NOUN _____

ADJECTIVE _____

VERB ENDING IN "ING" _____

ARTICLE OF CLOTHING _____

A PLACE _____

TYPE OF CONTAINER _____

TYPE OF FOOD _____

A PLACE _____

OCCUPATION _____

PART OF THE BODY _____

TYPE OF EVENT _____

CELEBRITY _____

VERB _____

TYPE OF LIQUID _____

NUMBER _____

TYPE OF FOOD _____

ADJECTIVE _____

The key to creating a healthy _____ is planning

NOUN

ahead! Let's take a look at some _____ events in the

ADJECTIVE

week ahead. Day one begins with Richard's _____

VERB ENDING IN "ING"

class to get the blood pumping fast. Don't forget to bring an extra

_____ in case of too much sweat. After that, head

ARTICLE OF CLOTHING

back to (the) _____ to fix meals for the week. Each

A PLACE

_____ gets one serving of _____ . Yum! Day

TYPE OF CONTAINER TYPE OF FOOD

two begins with a visit to (the) _____ to work with a

A PLACE

professional _____ who makes sure your _____

OCCUPATION PART OF THE BODY

is in good shape. Day three is the _____ where

TYPE OF EVENT

_____ lets people _____ for prizes. Can't wait

CELEBRITY VERB

to get drenched in _____ . Day _____ is all

TYPE OF LIQUID NUMBER

about relaxing and eating _____ . We all deserve a/an

TYPE OF FOOD

_____ day of rest.

ADJECTIVE

MAD LIBS® is fun to play with friends, but you can also play it by yourself! To begin with, DO NOT look at the story on the page below. Fill in the blanks on this page with the words called for. Then, using the words you have selected, fill in the blank spaces in the story.

Now you've created your own hilarious MAD LIBS® game!

LETTER TO A LEGEND

LAST NAME _____

PERSON IN ROOM _____

ADJECTIVE _____

PLURAL NOUN _____

TYPE OF EVENT _____

VERB ENDING IN "ING" _____

VERB _____

CITY _____

A PLACE _____

PART OF THE BODY _____

TYPE OF FOOD _____

ADJECTIVE _____

PLURAL NOUN _____

EXCLAMATION _____

COLOR _____

ARTICLE OF CLOTHING _____

ADJECTIVE _____

CELEBRITY _____

Dear Mr. _____,
                 LAST NAME

May I call you _____? I'm so _____ right
              PERSON IN ROOM   ADJECTIVE

now! I've been such a big fan of yours ever since I watched your

video *Party Off the* _____. It looked like such a great
                  PLURAL NOUN

_____. Everyone was _____ and having
  TYPE OF EVENT   VERB ENDING IN "ING"

fun. I thought, *I want to* _____, *too!* So, I took a trip to
                   VERB

_____, walked right into (the) _____, and signed
   CITY   A PLACE

up for one of your famous workouts. I was so nervous that my

_____ started making noises as if I'd eaten some bad
PART OF THE BODY

_____. But then " _____ _____ of Fire"
  TYPE OF FOOD   ADJECTIVE   PLURAL NOUN

began to play, and I couldn't help but shout, " _____!"
                              EXCLAMATION

Everyone looked at me like I was wearing a/an _____
                                  COLOR

_____ on my head, but I didn't care. It was a/an
ARTICLE OF CLOTHING

_____ day—maybe the best day of my life. Thank you,
 ADJECTIVE

_____! You're fantastic.
 CELEBRITY

MAD LIBS® is fun to play with friends, but you can also play it by yourself! To begin with, DO NOT look at the story on the page below. Fill in the blanks on this page with the words called for. Then, using the words you have selected, fill in the blank spaces in the story.

Now you've created your own hilarious MAD LIBS® game!

YOU'RE DOING FANTASTIC

PERSON IN ROOM _____

TYPE OF FOOD _____

VERB _____

NUMBER _____

CELEBRITY _____

VERB ENDING IN "ING" _____

PART OF THE BODY _____

COLOR _____

ANIMAL _____

TYPE OF LIQUID _____

ADJECTIVE _____

ARTICLE OF CLOTHING _____

NOUN _____

VEHICLE _____

OCCUPATION _____

PART OF THE BODY _____

MAD LIBS

YOU'RE DOING FANTASTIC

Taylor: Thanks for inviting me to _____'s _____
PERSON IN ROOM   TYPE OF FOOD

Truck, but I don't know if I can _____ here. I'm on day
VERB

_____ of the _____ meal plan and exercise program.
NUMBER   CELEBRITY

Jordan: Me too! I've been _____ so much this week,
VERB ENDING IN "ING"

my _____ is tired. Ha-ha.
PART OF THE BODY

Taylor: I should probably get the _____ salad, but the
COLOR

_____ wings with a side of _____ look so
ANIMAL   TYPE OF LIQUID

_____. How's the program going for you?
ADJECTIVE

Jordan: I can fit into my old _____ again, so
ARTICLE OF CLOTHING

that's cool. But sometimes it's hard to get out of my queen-size

_____ in the morning.
NOUN

Taylor: I wish my bed was a/an _____! You know, I'm no
VEHICLE

_____, but if you ever need a workout partner, I've got your
OCCUPATION

_____.
PART OF THE BODY

MAD LIBS® is fun to play with friends, but you can also play it by yourself! To begin with, DO NOT look at the story on the page below. Fill in the blanks on this page with the words called for. Then, using the words you have selected, fill in the blank spaces in the story.

Now you've created your own hilarious MAD LIBS® game!

CHANGE OF HEART

VERB ENDING IN "ING" _____

CELEBRITY _____

PART OF THE BODY (PLURAL) _____

FIRST NAME _____

SOMETHING ALIVE (PLURAL) _____

ADJECTIVE _____

PERSON IN ROOM _____

NUMBER _____

A PLACE _____

TYPE OF LIQUID _____

PLURAL NOUN _____

ANIMAL (PLURAL) _____

OCCUPATION _____

ARTICLE OF CLOTHING (PLURAL) _____

VERB ENDING IN "ING" _____

PLURAL NOUN _____

ADJECTIVE _____

SAME PERSON IN ROOM _____

MAD LIBS®

CHANGE OF HEART

A bunch of people _____ to _____ songs
_____(VERB ENDING IN "ING")_____(CELEBRITY)

and shaking their _____ just isn't my thing.
_____(PART OF THE BODY (PLURAL))

When I first heard about _____'s famous exercise class
_____(FIRST NAME)

from all my _____ , it sounded so _____.
_____(SOMETHING ALIVE (PLURAL))_____(ADJECTIVE)

_____ told me I would have fun, so I showed up at
(PERSON IN ROOM)

_____ o'clock in the morning at (the) _____ with my
(NUMBER)_____(A PLACE)

_____ in hand. There were _____ everywhere,
(TYPE OF LIQUID)_____(PLURAL NOUN)

taking selfies and acting like _____. Not my style at all.
_____(ANIMAL (PLURAL))

But then the _____ played "These _____
_____(OCCUPATION)_____(ARTICLE OF CLOTHING (PLURAL))

Were Made for _____," and I felt my body come
_____(VERB ENDING IN "ING")

alive. Everyone danced like their _____ depended on it!
_____(PLURAL NOUN)

At the end of the class, Richard told me I was a/an _____
_____(ADJECTIVE)

dancer. I guess _____ was right all along.
_____(SAME PERSON IN ROOM)

From RICHARD SIMMONS MAD LIBS® • © Jemini LLC.
Published by Mad Libs, an imprint of Penguin Random House LLC, 2022

MAD LIBS® is fun to play with friends, but you can also play it by yourself! To begin with, DO NOT look at the story on the page below. Fill in the blanks on this page with the words called for. Then, using the words you have selected, fill in the blank spaces in the story.

Now you've created your own hilarious MAD LIBS® game!

DANCE YOUR PANTS OFF

ADJECTIVE _____

SILLY WORD _____

LAST NAME _____

PART OF THE BODY _____

A PLACE _____

NOUN _____

TYPE OF FOOD (PLURAL) _____

ADJECTIVE _____

VERB _____

SILLY WORD _____

NOUN _____

PERSON IN ROOM _____

ADJECTIVE _____

ARTICLE OF CLOTHING (PLURAL) _____

ADJECTIVE _____

PLURAL NOUN _____

How well do you know Richard's famous workouts and exercise programs? Take this quiz and find out!

1. What was the first name of Richard's _____ studio?
   ADJECTIVE

   (a) The _____ Studio, (b) _____'s Workout
   SILLY WORD   LAST NAME

   Hut, (c) The Funny _____, (d) Anatomy
   PART OF THE BODY

   _____
   A PLACE

2. Which of these is *not* the name of one of Richard's books?

   (a) _____ *Pie: The Richard Simmons Private Collection*
   NOUN

   of Dazzling _____, (b) *Still* _____ *After*
   TYPE OF FOOD (PLURAL)   ADJECTIVE

   All These Years: My Story, (c) _____ *-a-Meal Cook Book*,
   VERB

   (d) *The* _____ *Body* _____
   SILLY WORD   NOUN

3. _____ is also known for which of the following things:
   PERSON IN ROOM

   (a) wearing _____ _____, (b)
   ADJECTIVE   ARTICLE OF CLOTHING (PLURAL)

   his _____ hair, (c) donating _____ to people
   ADJECTIVE   PLURAL NOUN

   in need, (d) all of the above

If you answered *d* to all these questions, you're a real Richard Simmons fan!

From RICHARD SIMMONS MAD LIBS® • © Jemini LLC.
Published by Mad Libs, an imprint of Penguin Random House LLC, 2022

MAD LIBS® is fun to play with friends, but you can also play it by yourself! To begin with, DO NOT look at the story on the page below. Fill in the blanks on this page with the words called for. Then, using the words you have selected, fill in the blank spaces in the story.

Now you've created your own hilarious MAD LIBS® game!

I'M PROUD OF YOU

VERB (PAST TENSE) _____

SILLY WORD _____

PART OF THE BODY _____

NUMBER _____

VERB ENDING IN "ING" _____

ARTICLE OF CLOTHING _____

CELEBRITY _____

ADJECTIVE _____

TYPE OF FOOD _____

VERB _____

COUNTRY _____

ADJECTIVE _____

OCCUPATION _____

FIRST NAME _____

A PLACE _____

VERB _____

PLURAL NOUN _____

PERSON IN ROOM _____

MAD LIBS®

I'M PROUD OF YOU

Look at how much you've all _____! It may sound
VERB (PAST TENSE)

like a load of _____, but I knew deep down in my
SILLY WORD

_____ that you could do it. If I've said it once, I've
PART OF THE BODY

said it _____ times, _____ isn't about fitting
NUMBER VERB ENDING IN "ING"

into your _____ or looking like _____.
ARTICLE OF CLOTHING CELEBRITY

It's about being _____ and having fun! You can have
ADJECTIVE

that plate of _____, but you'll have to _____
TYPE OF FOOD VERB

for it. That's the deal. And remember there are tons of people across

_____ who are doing the same thing as you. Doesn't
COUNTRY

that make you feel _____? Listen, I'm not a fancy
ADJECTIVE

_____ or anything. I'm just little ol' _____ from
OCCUPATION FIRST NAME

(the) _____. But if I can _____ it, you can, too! Now
A PLACE VERB

go out there and treat _____ with respect and kindness,
PLURAL NOUN

okay? And don't forget to save some for _____.
PERSON IN ROOM